alive Natural Health Guides 30

Kathleen O'Bannon CNC

Sprouts

The savory source
for health and vitality

Vancouver
Canada

Contents

Note: Conversions in this book (from imperial to metric) are not exact. They have been rounded to the nearest measurement for convenience. Exact measurements are given in imperial. The recipes in this book are by no means to be taken as therapeutic. They simply promote the philosophy of both the author and *alive* books in relation to whole foods, health and nutrition, while incorporating the practical advice given by the author in the first section of the book.

Recipes

32   34   50   52

Sprouts offer a tremendous amount of life force and a powerhouse of nutrients.

Sprouts are vital and alive, as you will be when you eat them regularly.

Sprouts for Life . . . .

So many people today are suffering from fatigue, lack of energy, low self-esteem, and many degenerative diseases. In short, they feel bad most of the time. Does this sound familiar? There is another way to live. Adding whole, natural foods, including sprouts, to your diet and lifestyle is an easy way to gain energy and vitality.

Why eat sprouts? For many reasons–they are:
• healthy, economical and convenient
• packed with nutrition
• fresh, vital and alive all year round
• Inexpensive, fresh vegetables
• easy to grow at home by anybody.

Sprouts are a living food. When seeds sprout, a tremendous amount of life force is released and a powerhouse of nutrients becomes available to you. In the process, seeds attain a higher level of vitamins, and complex carbohydrates and proteins are converted into easily digestible forms. Sprouts contain enzymes–lots of them–which are the life element in our food and the sparkplugs to creating energy in every single cell of the body. Learning to take advantage of the incomparable nutritional power and living energy of sprouts will set you on a course for lifelong health.

Adding sprouts to your diet is an easy way to gain energy, vitality and good health.

Sprouts cure the winter "blahs." During winter, really fresh, nutritionally sound vegetables are often difficult to find in the supermarket. Often vegetables are shipped a long distance and devoid of nutritional value by the time you get them. Ta-da! Sprouts fill this gap. You can easily and inexpensively grow sprouts in any location.

I've grown and eaten sprouts for more than twenty years, so I can attest to the way sprouts lift my energy and spirits. When I first started eating sprouts, I couldn't find them in any stores, especially where I lived in Northern Ontario. Today, sprouts are found everywhere and recognized as an important nutrient-rich food to boost your immune system and protect against conditions such as aging, cancer, heart disease and obesity. What used to be called "rabbit food" is now becoming a commonplace staple in the kitchen and part of a healthful diet.

Digital Stock

7

Eating sprouts helps cure the winter blahs; and they are a fresh, live vegetable that's available year round.

Sprouts Then . . . .

Sprouts have been used for thousands of years as part of a healthful and healing lifestyle. The Chinese have been eating bean sprouts regularly since 3,000 BC, using them to help cure bloating, muscle cramps, loss of nerve sensation, digestive disorders and weakness of the lungs. An ancient, comprehensive work on Chinese pharmaceuticals and herbs talks about using sprouts to reduce inflammation, produce a laxative effect, cure rheumatism, and build and tone the body.

The Essenes, a religious sect of mystics living in the ancient Middle East around the beginning of our calendar, made their daily bread using sprouts. Essene bread, which is extremely easy to make (see page 46), is gaining popularity because it is not made with flour, and is therefore easy to digest. It is also yeast-free, for those who are on a yeast-free diet. Also, if you're trying to stay away from sugar, a sprouted grain bread like the essene bread is your answer, as it is naturally sweet. When wheat or another grain is sprouted, the starches in the grains are turned to sugars. Essene bread, made with raisins or other dried fruit, tastes like a very moist fruit cake.

Sprouts were also used to protect against scurvy, well before citrus fruits were discovered to provide the vitamin C needed to prevent the disease. During the eighteenth century, Captain James Cook formulated a sprouted bean malt and sailed with it for three years without losing a sailor to scurvy.

In more recent times, sprouts were considered one of the best and most economical ways to bring vitamin C-rich food to the frontlines during World War I. During a severe food shortage in India in the 1940s, people were given sprouts to eat, reducing deaths due to scurvy and starvation. And during World War II, sprouts were promoted in the US as an alternative source of protein.

> Let the angels of God prepare your bread. Moisten your wheat, that the angel of water may enter it. Then set it in the air, that the angel of air also may embrace it. And leave it from morning to evening beneath the sun, that the angel of sunshine may descend upon it. And the blessing of the three angels will soon make the germ of life to sprout your wheat.
> —From *The Essene Gospel of Peace* by Edmond Bordeaux Szekely

Sprouts Now . . . .

Today, sprouts are widely available in supermarkets and organic seeds for sprouting are commonplace in health food stores and in garden centers and other seed outlets. More and more people are eating sprouts, and finding that they supply the life force the body needs to heal and rejuvenate.

It's easy to eat fresh organically grown sprouts—just put them in or on everything! Garnish your soup or stew with sprouts just before serving. Top off every salad or sandwich with sprouts and add them to shakes and smoothies. They're delicious in cereal, with bagels and cream cheese, and in every sandwich you can think of. Chopped fresh sprouts and parsley make a wonderful garnish for all cooked food, adding flavor and freshness. Use this combination daily in place of salt and pepper and it will give you new-found energy. Eating sprouts regularly will soon change your life for the better.

Pioneers of Sprouting

I first found recipes for growing sprouts in a book by Beatrice Trum Hunter, one of the early pioneers of sprouts and sprouting. Beatrice Trum Hunter encouraged people to eat healthier and be in tune with the environment; it was because of her early books that I changed my life completely. I started to eat natural organic food, grow my own sprouts, and raise herbs and other organically grown vegetables. I made most of my own basic foods and raised goats and chickens. This lifestyle led to my opening a vegetarian cooking school, teaching natural food cooking and writing about it for over twenty-five years. Thank you Beatrice Trum Hunter.

Another important pioneer is Ann Wigmore, considered the mother of modern sprouting. She espoused sprouts to accompany a raw food diet for health and healing. In her clinics in Boston, The Ann Wigmore Foundation and The Hippocrates Institute, she taught people to eat sprouts along with a healthy diet of raw foods and wheat grass juice as part of her cures for many illnesses. Sprouting has become popular largely due to her tireless efforts.

Canadian pioneer in healthy eating Paavo Airola recommended sprouts as part of "The Airola Diet for Optimum Health, Youthful Vitality, and Long Life." Sprouts qualify as both seeds and vegetables, two of Airola's three basic food groups. He suggested sprouts for the raw, living food part of his diet and even said that sprouts contained complete protein because of the sprouting process. Many of his regimes for specific ailments emphasized plenty of sprouts and raw seeds, nuts, grains, fruits and vegetables.

For those who do not wish to grow their own sprouts, they are becoming widely available at markets and in grocery stores.

Powerhouse of Energy . . . .

When seeds sprout they unleash a powerhouse of vital nutrients to start the plant growing. Eating sprouts harnesses that vitality and living energy. People who eat live foods, especially fresh sprouts and raw organically grown vegetables, stay vital and youthful.

I once went to hear organic farmer and nurseryman John Tobe speak; he was so dynamic and vibrant that it was hard to believe he was over 70 years old at the time. He didn't have any wrinkles and even though he spoke in a large auditorium to more than 100 people, he didn't use a microphone and could be heard in every corner of the hall.

Tobe talked about growing and eating sprouts along with organic vegetables. That was when I realized that eating live food would make me lively.

If you have too little energy or feel tired in the afternoon, try adding live, vital sprouts to your meals every day and you will soon have a surprising increase in energy. They are alive and highly nutritious; in fact, no food offers more nutrition. Sprouts contain protein; vitamins A, B-complex, C, D and E; enzymes; iron; potassium; magnesium; calcium; phosphorus; trace elements such as zinc and chromium; amino acids; and essential fatty acids.

When seeds sprout they unleash a powerhouse of vital nutrients in order to start the growth process.

Cancer-Fighting Sprouts . . . .

Phytochemicals are a group of health-promoting nutrients that give plants their color, flavor and resistance to disease. Phytochemicals also protect the body against cancers. Genestein is found in soybeans and it prevents the formation of the capillaries needed to nourish tumors, thereby killing the tumors. The saponins found in kidney beans, chick peas, soybeans and lentils may even prevent cancer cells from multiplying.

Three-day old broccoli and cauliflower sprouts contain 10 to 100 times more glucoraphanin or sulforaphane than the mature plants do. These phytochemicals were very effective in reducing mammary tumors in a study conducted by the Johns Hopkins University School of Medicine. The study concludes that "a small amount of broccoli or cauliflower sprouts can protect against the risk of cancer as effectively as much larger amounts of mature vegetables of the same variety."

Another study pinpointed one more ingredient in the sprouts that arrested human breast cancer cells: indol-3-carbinol. This component found in the *Brassica* family of vegetables, which includes cabbage, broccoli, cauliflower and Brussels sprouts, was shown to suppress the growth of mammary tumor cells independent of estrogen receptor signaling. This is helpful for women who have estrogen-dominant breast cancers in their family. If you have breast cancer in your family, it would be wise to start eating broccoli or cauliflower sprouts every day as protection against this disease.

Studies have shown that broccoli and cauliflower sprouts provide protection against breast cancer.

Digital Vision

Disease Prevention . . . .

Vegetables and fruits have higher amounts of fiber than other foods and adding sprouts to your daily diet substantially increases your fiber intake. A study of 2,909 healthy adults (called the Coronary Artery Risk Development in Young Adults Study,) showed that dietary fiber may prevent high levels of insulin and obesity associated with insulin resistance. The study also concluded that high fiber intake had more importance in preventing cardiovascular disease than did dietary intake of fat, carbohydrate or protein.

> Canadian healthy eating pioneer Paavo Airola, believed nutrition was the single most important factor affecting health and disease.

In other words, eating fiber-rich foods every day helps prevent heart disease, type II diabetes and obesity. The US government suggests eating a daily minimum of five half-cup (125 ml) servings.

Add an extra cup of sprouts and you will get enough fiber to both prevent disease and increase energy. In addition, sprouts are reported to contain substances, called sterols and sterolins, which work to reduce cholesterol levels.

Support for Your Immune System . . . .

As a living food, sprouts provide the nutrients to support the immune system, strengthening your body's ability to fight off disease. The sprouts of oilseed, wild potato, lupins, fenugreek, wild barley, soybean and sunflower have been used for centuries to cure immune and autoimmune diseases.

One of the body's natural means of staying healthy is its ability to detoxify itself. A variety of cleansing sprouts and sprout juices stimulates the body to flush out toxic waste. Tangy sprouts such as alfalfa, clover, fenugreek and radish detoxify the body. Phytochemicals called indoles, found in cauliflower, broccoli, cabbage and Brussels sprouts, increase immune activity and make it easier for the body to excrete toxins. In addition, sprouts are a rich source of easily digestible protein that unlike protein from animal sources won't putrefy in the stomach and slow down your metabolism.

Enzyme-Rich Vitality . . . .

Enzymes are present in live, raw, natural foods and multiplied greatly in sprouts. Soaking and sprouting seeds starts a natural process that often increases the amount of enzymes by fifteen or more times. This is fantastic news because your body needs enzymes to work properly. Enzymes are the very basis of every chemical and mechanical action and reaction in your body, from digestion to the repair of damaged tissue. Without enzymes, efficient nutrient absorption is impossible and all metabolic functions slow down, making the body age faster and more susceptible to disease.

Sprouts are an excellent source of enzymes, which are the "sparks of life" and help fight degenerative diseases, such as cancer and arthritis.

Eating sprouts and other raw vegetables and fruits daily can give you the enzymes to put a spring in your step and twinkle in your eye, even in old age. Our bodies are programmed at birth to live for 120 years, but few people ever make it to that age. Why? In part, the modern lifestyle leads to an enzyme deficiency in the body, causing poor nutrition at the cellular level, resulting in ill health. Pollution, smoking tobacco, drinking alcohol to excess and eating denatured food (food with no life force left in it) depletes your store of enzymes. The stress reaction called "fight-or-flight" can reduce your enzymes and increase your need for more at the same time. Aging and injury increase your need for enzymes. Also, as we age our

Enzyme-Enhancers

Easily digested sprouts are called "enzyme-enhancers" by Dr. Anthony Cichoke (Dr. Enzyme), author of *The Complete Book of Enzyme Therapy* (Avery, 1999), because they provide the richest source of plant enzymes to aid digestion. Each plant contains the enzyme necessary for its own digestion (as long as it isn't destroyed by heat or light), and when eaten, this very enzyme also helps the body digest other foods.

bodies produce fewer enzymes so we need to take in more in our daily meals.

Eating enzyme-rich food saves the body from having to make enzymes, a process that depletes energy. Studies show that eating fresh, raw vegetables and fruits, including sprouts, can boost the body's enzyme supply and help fight degenerative diseases such as cancer and arthritis.

Enzymes are extremely sensitive to heat and cannot function once subjected to heat over 118°F (45°C). It is very important to always eat raw food every day! With the exceptions of soybean and kidney bean sprouts, which you should cook slightly, adding raw sprouts to every meal will supply the enzymes vital for a vibrant life.

Vitamins and Minerals in Sprouts . . . .

Seeds are packed with enough vitamins and minerals to initiate sprouting even before the roots pick up nutrients from the soil and the leaves photosynthesize sunlight into energy. The

The seeds used for sprouting are packed with so many vitamins and minerals that they initiate sprouting without picking up nutrients from soil.

Siegfried Gursche

content of many of these vitamins and minerals actually increase when the seeds are sprouted, making the sprouts a highly concentrated source of nutrients. Moreover, these nutrients are the freshest you can get, staying intact up to the time you start chewing. In contrast, other raw vegetables start losing their nutrients the moment they are cut or plucked from the field.

Sprouts are rich in the antioxidant vitamins A, C and E as well as B vitamins.

Sprouts supply vitamin A mainly in the form of beta-carotene, which is easily assimilated and non-toxic. In general sprouts contain most of the trace minerals. Read the *Encyclopedia of Natural Healing* (*alive* books, 1998) for more information on how these nutrients affect your health.

Sprouts also absorb minerals from water, so it is best to soak and rinse them using mineral-rich water rather than distilled water. In an Austrian study, three grains—the ancient Inca grain quinoa, wheat and buckwheat—all absorbed minerals from the water during soaking and sprouting. Quinoa had the highest rates of mineral uptake. It's also a good idea to include a small piece of kelp or wakame seaweed in the soaking and/or rinsing water to increase the mineral content of the finished sprouts.

For years people ate sprouts made from all these plants and stayed healthy, now scientists are finding out why.

A-Z Guide to Choosing Sprouts

Any seed that can be grown into nutritious plants can be sprouted and enjoyed. Almost all spouts are healthy, some taste great, others add fun to meals, and several common sprouts such as radish and mustard taste spicy. The variety is incredible!

There are many healthy sprouts to choose from. All add nutrition, taste and fun to meals.

Some seeds are trickier to sprout than others. For example, adzuki beans—small, nearly round, deep red beans used in Oriental cooking—are great for sprouting, but they need a weight put on them after the sprouts have started to grow. Flax seeds shouldn't be soaked or they turn gelatinous and won't sprout. They sprout best when put on a moist red clay pot and misted daily.

Here is a list of the most popular seeds for easy sprouting. I've listed the known nutrients in these sprouts and how they can treat illness. If a type of sprout has only a few nutrients listed, that is only because it hasn't been tested and written about, it may contain many more nutrients as yet undiscovered. Every year more and more phytochemicals are found in fruits, grains and vegetables–especially sprouts–that are good for you. Every type of fresh sprout contains a life force that is essential to well-being, and the main reason we eat sprouts is to gain energy and vitality from this life force.

Adzuki beans: **Vitamin:** C. **Mineral:** iron. Protein.

Alfalfa: **Vitamins:** A, B_1, B_3, B_5, B_6, B_{12}, C, D, E, K. **Minerals:** calcium, copper, potassium, magnesium, iron, selenium, zinc. **Protein:** about 4 percent. **Saponins:** help remove plaque from the arteries and lower cholesterol. **Plant sterols:** build up the immune system and lower cholesterol. **Chlorophyll:** helps control hot flashes and supports estrogenic functions. **Canavanine:** an amino acid that can protect against pancreatic, colon and leukemia cancers.

alfalfa seeds

Almond: **Vitamins:** B complex, E. **Minerals:** calcium, magnesium, potassium, selenium. Protein and fatty acids.

Arugula: Spicy flavor. **Vitamins:** A, C. **Minerals:** calcium, iron. Chlorophyll.

Barley: **Vitamins:** A, B complex, C, E. **Minerals:** calcium, iron, magnesium, phosphorus. Glucans: help lower cholesterol and build up the immune system.

Broccoli: Amino acids. Chlorophyll. **Sulforaphane and glucoraphanin (among other phytochemicals):** protect against cancers and harmful oxidation. Three-day-old sprouts contain 10 to 100 times more protection than do the mature plants. **Indole-3-carbinol:** protects against skin cancers, inhibits skin tumors and reduces breast tumors.

Cabbage: Amino acids. Chlorophyll. **Sulforaphane and**

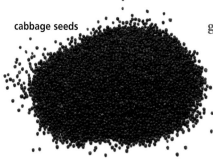
cabbage seeds

glucoraphanin (among other phytochemicals): protect against cancers and harmful oxidation in the body. Three-day-old sprouts contain 10 to 100 times more protection than do the mature plants. **Indole-3-carbinol:** protects against skin cancers, inhibits skin tumors and reduces breast tumors. Often used in combination with cabbage juice to reduce stomach ulcers.

Celery: Coumarins. Flavonoids. Essential fatty acids. Used to clear up skin problems. Useful for bronchitis, rheumatism, and nervousness.

Chick peas (also called cici or garbanzo beans): **Vitamin:** C. **Minerals:** iron, calcium, magnesium. Protein.

Clover (also called red clover): **Vitamins:** A, C. Phytochemicals that protect against disease. **Protein:** 4 percent. Chlorophyll if leaves turn green.

Coriander (also called cilantro, Chinese parsley): The seeds have been used extensively in Ayurvedic and Chinese medicine for hundreds of years. Sprouting the seeds increases the effectiveness. Used for griping, colic, indigestion, intestinal disorders, skin/rash problems (applied externally as a poultice), stomach ache, cleaning the breath and reversing halitosis.

Cow peas (also called black-eyed peas): **Vitamin:** C. **Mineral:** potassium.

Daikon (Japanese radish): Phytochemicals that protect against disease. In Chinese medicine: clears toxins from the liver.

Fennel: A favorite of Hildegard of Bingen, used for wasting problems and fatigue.

Fenugreek (also spelled foenugreek): **Vitamin:** A. **Mineral:** iron. Protein. **Saponins:** sterols and sterolins that inhibit intestinal absorption of cholesterol. In folk medicine used to expel mucus from the intestines. In India it is called methi and often used to reduce blood sugar in insulin-dependent diabetics.

Flax: **Vitamins:** A, B_1, B_2, C, D, E. **Essential fats:** alpha-linolenic acid (omega-3) and linoleic acid (omega-6). Improves functioning of all organs in the body. Phytoestrogens (plant estrogens) called lignans that help prevent breast, prostate, uterus and colon cancers.

Garlic: **Vitamins:** A, C. Contains antiviral, antibiotic and anti-fungal agents. Used to treat respiratory infections and the flu. Allylic sulfides known to protect against cancer. Reduces total cholesterol and triglycerides.

Kale: **Vitamins:** A, C, K. Similar properties to other members of the cabbage family. Do not eat raw.

Kidney beans: **Vitamin:** B complex. **Minerals:** calcium, potassium, iron. Do not eat raw.

Lentil (green and red): **Vitamins:** folic acid, C, E. **Minerals:** iron, phosphorus, potassium. Protein approximately 24 percent. Phytates that hinder the development of cancer.

Mung beans: **Vitamins:** A, C. **Minerals:** phosphorus, iron. Used in Oriental medicine for cooling purposes in diseases where there is heat.

Mustard seeds: **Vitamin:** A. Spicy addition to foods.

Nettles (often called stinging nettles): **Vitamin:** C. Protein. Contain the indoles histamine and serotonin which are useful for preventing seasonal allergies.

Oats: **Vitamin:** E. Proteins. Beta glucan used in building up the immune system and treating skin disorders, especially dry skin. Helpful in reducing cholesterol and triglycerides.

Onion: **Vitamins:** A, C. Contains antiviral, antibiotic and anti-fungal agents. Used to treat respiratory infections and the flu. Allylic sulfides known to protect against cancer. Reduces total cholesterol and triglycerides.

Peas: **Vitamin:** A. **Minerals:** iron, potassium, magnesium. Contain all eight essential amino acids and 22 percent protein.

Pumpkin seeds: **Vitamin:** B complex. **Mineral:** zinc. Especially useful for diseases of the prostate.

mung bean

quinoa

Quinoa: Vitamins: B_1, B_2, B_3, B_6, folacin. **Minerals:** copper, iron, magnesium, manganese, phosphorus, potassium, zinc. Protein.

Radish: Vitamins: A, C. More than 29 times the vitamin C and 4 times the vitamin A of milk. **Mineral:** calcium. **Protein:** 4 percent.

Rye: Vitamins: B complex, E. **Minerals:** magnesium, phosphorus, potassium. Protein.

Sesame seeds: Vitamins: B complex, E. **Mineral:** calcium, iron, magnesium, phosphorus, potassium. Fiber.

Soybeans: Vitamins: A, B_1, B_2, B_3, E. **Minerals:** calcium, phosphorus, iron, potassium. **Phytoestrogens:** increase bone density and prevent bone breakdown (osteoporosis). Helpful for premenstrual syndrome (PMS), menopause, hot flashes and fibrocystic breast disease. Do not eat raw.

Sunflower seeds: Vitamins: B complex, D, E. **Minerals:** calcium, iron, phosphorus, potassium, magnesium. Unsaturated fatty acids including omega-6. **Protein:** 4 percent.

Turnip seeds: Spicy addition to any food.

Watercress: Vitamins: A, C. **Minerals:** calcium, iron, potassium. Chlorophyll if leaves are green.

Wheat: Vitamins: B complex, E, folacin. **Minerals:** iron, magnesium, manganese. Carbohydrates, protein and omega-6 fatty acids.

soy beans

With so many sprouts to choose from, there's no reason to tire of this exciting and energizing food. Pumpkin seed spouts, for example, go wonderfully with both fruit and vegetables; sunflower sprouts are excellent in a summer salad; and soybean sprouts add both taste and nutrition to a stir fry when added just before removing from heat.

Buying Seeds for Sprouting . . . .

The seeds you choose to sprout will be determined by a few different factors: how and why you want to eat them, which seeds are available, and how much time you have to sprout them.

Many commercial seeds are coated with various chemicals to keep them from sprouting too soon, to keep pests away, and to prevent blight or mildew from forming on them. The seeds and nuts that are found in the food section of a natural food store are more likely to sprout and will be safer for you to eat. (See the "Sources" section for places to find hard-to-get seeds).

Sprouts are the most healthful when grown from certified organically raised seeds. Many health food stores and seed outlets carry organic seeds specifically for sprouting.

20

Low-Cost, High-Quality Nutrients
Sprouts supply the highest quality nutrients at the lowest cost compared to the nutrients you get from most other foods. They especially make extremely economical winter greens when you grow them at home. Three to four ounces (100 grams) of small seeds will produce up to 20 cups (5 quarts or 5 liters) of sprouts.

When looking at the seeds, check the number of broken seeds. Broken seeds or beans will not sprout. The more whole seeds there are, the more sprouts you will have and the better the quality of seeds.

You want wheat, rye and oats with a natural coating on them. You don't want grains with a hull or husk on them, however, as they are too difficult to digest. Purchase seeds that are for sprouting and you will have no problems. While it's not impossible to sprout grains that have a hull or husk on them, it is time-consuming and offers no nutritional value.

Growing Your Own Sprouts
It's Easy! It's Healthy! . . . .

Sprouts are available in most salad bars, supermarkets and health food stores, but they are easy and fun to grow yourself. Your whole family can get involved in growing sprouts–children love to watch the little seeds sprout. Once again, make sure you use organically raised sprouting seeds.

Hydroponics

Sprouts don't need soil to grow. Growing sprouts in water, not soil, is often called "hydroponic" growing. A true hydroponic

Sprouts do not need soil to grow.

garden or farm would have the seeds soaking in water constantly. That is only because they want the plant to grow beyond the sprout stage. For growing sprouts, you add water and drain it off until the sprouts form; they shouldn't be sitting in water.

Simple, Easy and Inexpensive

I find the jar the easiest, simplest, and least expensive way to make sprouts: a wide-mouth glass jar with a nylon screen, cheesecloth or J-cloth over the neck. The sprouts grow perfectly and the jar is easy to clean when I'm done. Many hardware or kitchen supply stores sell gallon jars that are suitable for making your own sprouts at home.

Modern Sprouters

Of course, in our modern times we have many kinds of very efficient sprouters available. They are easy to use and some are even automatic, requiring less rinsing than the basic jar method. While I prefer the jar method for making small batches of several different seeds, the commercially manufactured sprouters are great for making a large batch of one type of seed.

Many of the sprouters have stacked trays so you can make several large batches of different sprouts at one time, allowing you to soak seeds and sprout them on separate layers and on different days and to rinse the layers at the same time. If you keep rotating the sprouts like this, you will always have on hand fresh sprouts of one kind or another.

A favorite sprouter is the EASY-SPROUT™. The sprouter's dual-container system uses heat from the sprouting seeds to circulate fresh, humidified air by natural convection. This system prevents suffocation and dehydration so sprouts need less rinsing than most sprouters; or as in the case of many types of seeds no rinsing is needed at all. Apart from the fact that it is truly quick and easy its unique design and the short time needed to sprout prevents the development of the mold that often turns people off sprouting. Check the "Sources" list at the back of the book for ordering information.

Step-by-Step Sprouting . . . .

By using just a few basic supplies and following a few easy steps, you can harvest fresh sprouts in your kitchen any time of the year.

> ### Sprouting Supplies
> These are the basic supplies you need to get started:
> - Organic sprouting seeds
> - Measuring spoons
> - Large wide-mouth jars with screens/cheesecloth/J-cloths or a sprouter
> - Cool, dry, very clean place

Sprouts grow best when stored in a cool, dry, clean place. A cupboard at below room temperature is fine, but make sure that it is not too cold for the sprouts to grow. The cupboard under the kitchen sink is often a great place, as long as it is clean. Wipe it down first and put the sprouts on a plate to avoid any contamination. Don't grow sprouts under the sink if you keep cleaning products there because they might pick up something toxic from the cleaners.

Basic Sprouting Method

Wash your hands thoroughly before handling any seeds, jars or other sprouting equipment, especially before stirring, rinsing or sorting the seeds or sprouts.

Step 1: Remove and discard any hulls, broken or discolored seeds, as well as any twigs or stones.

Step 2: Wash seeds carefully without breaking them.

Step 3: Place seeds in a jar or bowl and add cool water to soak. Generally add four times as much water as the volume of the seeds. For example, if you have 2 tablespoons (30 ml) of seeds, add at least 1/2 cup (125 ml) of water. If you want to increase the mineral content of your sprouts, add a piece of kelp or wakame seaweed to the soak water.

Step 4: Soak for the time mentioned in the sprouting chart (see pages 26 to 29) for each type of sprout (generally from six to twelve hours).

Step 5: Cover the jar with the screen and drain all the water off the seeds or drain the seeds and put them in the sprouter. Shake the jar to spread the seeds out and place it on its side at a 45°

Sprouting seeds is so easy it can even be done in a jar.

angle so that excess water can run off. Place the jar or sprouter in a cool, dark, clean place.

Step 6: Rinse and drain the sprouts three times daily using cool water. Generally, rinse once in the morning, once at noon or early evening, and then just before bedtime. You may also use a sprayer to moisten the seeds or sprouts. Always drain off all the excess water and shake the jar so that the seeds are evenly spread out and place the jar on its side.

Step 7: Once the sprouts have formed, expose them to indirect sunlight for one or two days or until the little leaves turn green. Direct sunlight is too hot for sprouts and may even cook them. (With alfalfa sprouts, expose them to the light for the last two days of growing, bringing them out into daylight as soon as the little leaves start to form.)

Step 8: Place finished sprouts in a large bowl of cool water and stir them around with your clean hand. This will allow the hulls and skins to come to the top and separate so you can remove them from the sprouts. Drain the remaining sprouts and put them in a bowl. They are ready to eat! Store them in the refrigerator for seven to ten days.

Growing Sprouts in Soil

The soil method of growing sprouts begins the same way as the jar method but the little sprouts are transferred to a tray or nursery flat filled with soil. They are grown indoors until the sprout is ready, a process that takes from five to fourteen days. Wheatgrass, sunflower and buckwheat sprouts are grown using the soil method.

Unhulled (in-shell) sunflower seeds grown in soil yields the delicious 4-inch (10 cm) long green sunflower sprouts. Once the seeds have soaked and sprouted a tiny tail in a jar, transfer them to the soil, where they'll be ready in five to eight days. You can also sprout hulled sunflower seeds using the jar method.

When Seeds Won't Sprout

Once in a while you'll find a batch of seeds that won't sprout. The seeds may be old or have been exposed to too much heat or moisture. Most oats, for example, are processed to prevent rancidity and extend shelf life. Unfortunately the vital life force has also been processed out of them.

Polished grains such as rice, pearl barley, oats or quinoa, will not sprout. Whole grains are generally not all the same color, while polished grains all look exactly the same. The quinoa from the Andean Partnership might be the only quinoa that is not polished, so look for this kind if you want to sprout quinoa.

Check your technique. You may have soaked for too little or too long a time, used contaminated water or provided too little ventilation. Make sure insects haven't damaged the seeds. Finally, let your source know if your seeds consistently won't sprout.

There are many kinds of efficient sprouters on the market to suit the needs of various consumers.

Item to be Sprouted	Method	Amount	Soaking Time
Adzuki Bean	Jar	½ cup	12 Hours
Alfalfa Seed	Jar	3 tablespoons	5 hours
Almond	Jar	3 cups	overnight (8–10 hours)
Amaranth	Jar	1 cup	3–5 hours
Barley (hulless variety)	Jar	1 cup	6 hours
Barley–unhulled, for grass	Soil–see Wheatgrass	2–2½ cups per flat	—
Broccoli seed	Jar	2 tablespoons	8 hours
Buckwheat, hulled	Jar	1 cup	6 hours (no longer)
Buckwheat, unhulled	Soil–see Wheatgrass	2–2½ cups per flat	—
Cabbage seed	Jar	1 tablespoon	4–6 hours
Clover	Jar	3 tablespoons	5 hours
Fenugreek	Jar	4 tablespoons	6 hours
Garbanzo Bean (also called chick pea or cici bean)	Jar	1 cup	12–48 hours
Kale seed	Jar	4 tablespoons	4–6 hours
Kamut	Jar or soil	—	—
Lentil	Jar	¾ cup	8 hours
Mustard seed	Jar	3 tablespoons	5 hours

Sprouting Time	Special Instructions	Estimated Yield	Length at Harvest
3–5 Days	Rinse 2–3 times a day.	4 cups	½"–1½" (1 cm–3.5cm)
3–6 days	Grows rapidly in warm climates; 'green' in indirect sun on last day.	3–4 cups	1"–2" (2.5cm–5cm)
Most often used soaked only–can be sprouted 1–2 days	Will keep in refrigerator up to 5 days–change soak water daily.	4 cups	0–⅛" (up to 0.25 cm)
2–3 days	Rinse 3 or more times a day.	3 cups	0–¼" (up to 0.5cm)
12–24 hours	Difficult to obtain viable hulless variety for jar sprouting.	2½ cups	0–¼" (up to 0.5cm)
7–10 days	Follow instructions for wheatgrass.	—	—
3–4 days	Rinse 2–3 times a day. Iin indirect sun last 1–2 days.	2 cups	1"–2" (2.5cm–5cm)
1–2 days	For best results, rinse every 30 minutes for the first few hours.	2 cups	⅛"–½" (0.25cm–1cm)
7–9 days	Follow instructions for wheatgrass.	—	—
4–5 days	Rinse 2–3 times a day, shaking vigorously.	1½ cups	1"–2" (2.5cm–5cm)
4–6 days	Grows rapidly in warm climates, 'green' in indirect sun on last day.	3–4 cups	1"–2" (2.5cm–5cm)
2–5 days	Becomes bitter if left to grow past one inch.	2½–3 cups	1"–2" (2.5cm–5cm)
2–4 days	Soak longer for easier digestion. Rinse often.	3–3½ cups	½"–1" (1 cm–2.5cm)
4–6 days	Rinse 2–3 times a day.	3–4 cups	¾"–1" (1.5cm–2.5 cm)
—	Follow instructions for wheatgrass.	—	—
2–3 days	Grows rapidly in warm climates. Rinse often. Use whole, unbroken, unsplit lentils.	3–4 cups	½"–1" (1 cm–2.5cm)
3–5 days	In indirect sun on last day.	3 cups	½"–1½" (1 cm–3.5cm)

Item to be Sprouted	Method	Amount	Soaking Time
Oats, hulled (unhulled for oat milk only)	Jar	1 cup	8 hours
Onion seed	Jar	1 tablespoon	4–6 hours
Pea	Jar	1 cup	8 hours
Pea (Pea Shoot)	Soil–see Wheatgrass	—	—
Pinto Bean	Jar	1 cup	12 hours
Pumpkin	Jar	1 cup	6 hours
Quinoa	Jar	1 cup	3–4 hours
Radish	Jar	3 tablespoons	6 hours
Rye	Jar	1 cup	6–8 hours
Seseame seed, hulled*	Jar	1 cup	8 hours
Sesame seed, unhulled*	Jar	1 cup	4–6 hours
Spelt	Jar	1 cup	6 hours
Sunflower, hulled	Jar	1 cup	6–8 hours
Sunflower, unhulled	Soil–see Wheatgrass	2–2½ cups per flat	—
Teff	Jar	1 cup	3–4 hours
Wheat (for sprouts)	Jar	1 cup	8–10 hours
Wheatgrass–(Red winter wheat is the most commonly used variety)	Soil	2 cups per nursery flat	Soak in jar or bucket for 8–12 hours. Important to transfer sprouts to damp soil prior to reaching ¼"(0.5cm).

Estimated yield: these are rough approximations, there are too many variables to be accurate.
*Hulled sesame seed: will not sprout. Soak for 8 hours prior to using.
*Unhulled sesame seed: will sprout, good for sesame milk, strain very carefully. As sprouts, hulls are irritating to digestive tract for some people.

Sprouting Time	Special Instructions	Estimated Yield	Length at Harvest
1–2 days	Rinse 3 times a day. Buy unsteamed. Difficult to sprout; usually to use soaked only.	1 cup	0–⅛" (up to 0.25 cm)
4–5 days	Rinse 3 times a day.	1½–2 cups	1"–2" (2.5 cm– 5 cm)
2–3 days	Refrigerate at ½"(1cm). Will keep 7–14 days if rinsed and drained regularly.	2½ cups	½"–1" (1 cm – 2.5 cm)
10–14 days	Follow instructions for wheatgrass.	—	4"–7" (10 cm–17.5 cm)
3–4 days	Rinse 4 times a day or more.	3–4 cups	½"–1" (1 cm – 2.5 cm)
1–2 days	May not grow a sprout. Okay to use after soaking only.	1½–2 cups	0–⅛" (up to 0.25 cm)
2–3 days	For better taste-rinse 5–6 times prior to soaking.	3 cups	0–½" (up to 1 cm)
3–5 days	Rinse often and drain well. Needs air circulation. 'Green' in sun on last day.	3–4 cups	¾"–2" (1.5 cm–5 cm)
2–3 days	Rinse 2 times a day. Do not leave in an overly warm environment.	3 cups	½"–¾" (1cm–1.5cm)
—	Soak 8 hours, no sprouting.	1½ cups	will not sprout
1–2 days	Rinse 4 times a day.	1½ cups	0–⅛" (up to 0.25 cm)
1–2 days	Use in recipes in place of wheat.	—	0–¼" (up to 0.5cm)
less than one day	Skim off skins after soaking.	2 cups	¼"– ½" (0.5 cm –1cm)
5–8 days	Follow instructions for wheatgrass.	—	—
1–2 days	—	2½–3 cups	0–⅛" (up to 0.25 cm)
2–3 days	Grows rapidly in warm climates.	2–3 cups	¼"–¾" (0.5cm–1.5cm)
Place empty flat on top of seedlings. Leave alone. In 2–3 days, spouts will lift up the top tray. Harvest between day 8 and10. Second growth possible, but not as sweet or as nourishing. Directions vary according to climate.	Days 3–8 water but do not soak the soil. Allow sprouts ample light to green. Put outdoors in the day during warm weather, or use a grow light or southern exposure window. Harvest before second set of leaves. Cut and store in refrigerator; keeps 5–7 days.	—	—

The Raw Gourmet by Nomi Shannon (*alive* books, 1999)

Unless otherwise indicated, all jar sprouts should be rinsed 2 or 3 times a day. Directions: Fill jar with water. Swish vigorously, drain, repeat. All jar sprouts should be inverted in a dish rack or similar rack while sprouting. All jar sprouts require air circulation while sprouting and are best covered with screening, cheesecloth, or special sprouting lids.

Unleash a powerhouse of
vital nutrients—eat sprouts!

Tomato-Sprout Energy Smoothie

Sprouts are not just for salads. With some imagination and determination this high-energy food can be enjoyed throughout the day–even for breakfast! You'll have a great day when you take in the energy, antioxidants and many other nutrients in this vital (and tasty) smoothie.

2 lbs (1 kg) **large ripe tomatoes, cut in chunks**

2 cups (500 ml) **mixed sprouts, such as alfalfa, pumpkin and sunflower**

Herbamare, to taste

Purée tomatoes and sprouts in a blender until smooth. Season with Herbamare and serve.

Variation: Add 1 cup (250 ml) of diced celery and blend until smooth.

Serves 2

Herbamare

tomato

Herbamare
This tasty natural seasoning is made with sea salt and 14 organic herbs. The special steeping process used to make this natural product allows the full herb and vegetable flavor to become concentrated in the salt crystal–preserving essential vitamins and minerals and providing ultimate zest.

Carrot-Sunflower Sprout Muffins

This is a hearty snack, or a part of a complete breakfast, filled with phytonutrients, vitamin E and beta-carotene. These muffins can help prevent PMS and menopause symptoms when added to your diet on a regular basis along with other soy foods. They are great served with kefir, yogurt or natural cheese.

2 cups (500 ml) **carrots, finely grated**

½ cup (125 ml) **extra-virgin olive or unrefined sunflower oil**

2 tbsp water

2 organic eggs, beaten

2 tsp pure vanilla extract

¼ cup (60 ml) **organic soy grits or okara**

2 cups (500 ml) **organic whole wheat pastry flour**

2 tsp ground cinnamon

1 tbsp baking soda

⅔ cup (165 ml) **natural sugar** (Rapadura or Sucanat)

⅔ cup (165 ml) **sunflower seed sprouts, chopped**

1 cup (250 ml) **organic raisins or currants**

Preheated oven to 325°F (160°C).

In a bowl, combine carrots, oil, water, eggs and vanilla extract. Sift in soy grits, flour, cinnamon, baking soda and sugar. Add sprouts and raisins; mix gently. Spoon mixture into lined muffin pans. Bake for 35 minutes (less for regular or medium muffins). Insert a toothpick or tester into the muffin; if it comes out clean, the muffins are done. Do not overcook or the muffins will be dry.

Makes 6 giant, or 12 medium, muffins

What's Okara?
Okara is the soy pulp that remains after soy milk is squeezed out of soy mash used to make tofu or soy milk. If you make your own tofu you might have this on hand in your freezer.

Natural Sugar
Natural sugar crystals may be equally substituted for the white sugar called in your recipes. There are many types of natural sugar crystals on the market. Some are superior to others simply because of the way they're made. I use either Sucanat or Rapadura. These natural sweeteners have a higher nutritional value than white sugar, with a natural rich flavor. Unlike the process used to make white refined sugar, the process used to make these natural sugars preserves the natural taste and nutrition, without preservatives or additives, and actually has a lower level of sucrose than refined sugar.

Cleansing Sprout and Daikon Salad

In Chinese medicine, daikon clears the liver of toxins. Savory sprouts such as alfalfa, clover, fenugreek and radish also help detoxify the body. Everyone needs to cleanse once in a while, especially if you eat any type of processed food or animal proteins; and also if you live or work near air or water pollution.

2 cups (500 ml) **daikon radish, shredded**

1 cup (250 ml) **fenugreek sprouts**

½ cup (125 ml) **celery seed sprouts**

½ cup (125 ml) **clover sprouts**

½ cup (125 ml) **daikon or other radish sprouts**

¼ cup (60 ml) **extra-virgin olive oil**

2 tbsp fresh lemon juice

2 tsp fresh ginger, grated

Herbamare or sea salt and fresh ground pepper, to taste

In a large bowl, whisk together oil, lemon juice, ginger and seasoning. Add daikon and sprouts, toss well and serve.

Serves 2

ginger

lemon

First on the Menu

A salad can be a meal in itself, but when you do plan to eat another course, the salad should always be eaten first. Salads, especially a salad with powerhouse nutrients such as sprouts in it, will stimulate the body's digestive enzymes and also provide extra enzymes, which will help you digest your meal better.

Sprout-Avocado
Salad with Goat Cheese

This salad is a real winner and a balanced meal in itself. The good and healthful fats in walnuts and avocado, and the many nutrients and enzymes in the sprouts, help fight degenerative diseases such as cancer and arthritis. Aside from an amazing combination of nutrients and taste, this meal will definitely boost energy levels.

2 cups (500 ml) **mixed alfalfa, sunflower or sprouts of your choice**

1 ripe avocado, cut in half

2 tsp fresh lemon juice

¼ cup (60 ml) **walnuts**

2 ripe tomatoes, cut in wedges

½ cup (125 ml) **dried organic apricots**

½ lb (250 g) **goat cheese**

2 tsp fresh herbs, such as rosemary or thyme, chopped

2 tsp chives, chopped

In a small bowl, combine goat cheese and herbs. Place sprouts onto plates, arrange avocado on top and drizzle with lemon juice. Spoon goat cheese-herb mixture in the center of the avocado and garnish with walnuts. Arrange tomato and apricot around and serve.

Serves 2

avocado

Purchasing Tip
When buying an avocado choose a firm one with rough skin and a greenish tint. The avocado ripens after it's picked from the tree. Only buy a ripe avocado if you plan to use it right away.

Happy Digesting
Goat's cheese is more easily digested than cheese made from cow's milk. Aside from its healthful benefits, goat's milk adds a different touch to just about any salad as it has the perfect taste and consistency for the job.

Asian Sprout Salad

Soybean sprouts are a staple in the Asian diet. Look for them, along with baby corn and watercress, in Asian food stores. This salad is both healthful and stylish. Served to dinner guests, it will boost their health and your reputation as an imaginative and talented host. The dressing lends a unique taste to an already delicious salad and it's easy to make.

6–8 baby carrots	**Dressing:**
8–10 stalks asparagus	**½ cup** (125 ml) **sesame seed oil**
2 cups (500 ml) **soybean sprouts**	**½ cup** (125 ml) **rice wine vinegar**
	¼ cup (60 ml) **tamari or teriyaki sauce**
1 cup (250 ml) **watercress**	**2 tbsp cold-pressed pumpkin seed oil**
1 cup (250 ml) **baby corn, cut ½"** (1 cm)	**1 tbsp honey**
	1 ½ tsp fresh cilantro, chopped
	2 tsp fresh lime juice
	1 tsp garlic, minced
	1 tsp sesame seeds
	½ tsp cracked chili
	Zest of a lime (optional)

Sesame Seeds
Asian recipes often call for this under appreciated seed. The sesame seed may be small, but it packs a powerful punch when it comes to nutrition and taste. It is rich in calcium, potassium, iron, phosphorus and protein. When buying sesame seeds to add to your favorite recipes, make sure they are light in color.

In a pot of boiling salted water, blanch the carrots for 2 minutes, add asparagus and blanch for 3 minutes longer. Drain and immediately rinse with cold water.

In a bowl, whisk together dressing ingredients. In a separate bowl, combine sprouts, watercress and baby corn; add half the dressing and toss well. Arrange carrots and asparagus onto plates, drizzle with remaining dressing, place salad over top and serve.

Serves 2

40

Zucchini-Sprout
Soup with Roasted Garlic

The protein in sprouts is easily digested and won't putrefy in your stomach and slow down metabolism. Paired up with the almighty zucchini, this soup delivers taste and nutrition the body will love. In fact, the roasted garlic makes this soup heavenly.

3 large onions, sliced

¼ cup (60 ml) **butter**

4 cups (1 l) **zucchini, grated**

1 potato, peeled and sliced

4 tsp fresh basil, chopped

2 tsp fresh oregano, chopped

4 cups (1 l) **vegetable stock or water**

1 cup (250 ml) **kefir or buttermilk**

1 bulb garlic (not one single clove, but a whole bulb of them)

1 tbsp extra-virgin olive oil

1 tsp fresh thyme, chopped

1 ½ cups (375 ml) **sunflower sprouts** (or any other type of sprouts)

Sea salt and pepper

Herbamare, to taste

Fresh basil, for garnish

Sauté onion in butter for 5 minutes until tender. Add zucchini, potato and herbs and cook on low heat for 5 minutes. Stir in vegetable stock and slowly simmer for 10 minutes. Add buttermilk and heat until warmed through.

In the meantime, preheat oven to 375°F (190°C). Cut ½" (1 cm) off the top of the garlic bulb, rub with oil, sprinkle with thyme, salt and pepper then roast in the oven for 30 minutes, or until the tips of the cloves pop out of the skin. Remove from oven and squeeze the cloves out of the skins.

Blend soup, roasted garlic and sprouts in a blender until smooth. Return to pot and season. Heat on low until warmed through then garnish with fresh basil and serve.

Serves 6

Cooking with Butter

Yes, butter is better than margarine and cooking with it is a great idea. But be sure that you don't heat the butter to the point where it is brown. It's at this point that the butter (as with any fat heated past a certain point) becomes carcinogenic, which means it is not healthy and can even contribute to the development of cancer. For more information read *Good Fats and Oils* by Siegfried Gursche (*alive* Natural Health Guide #17, 2000).

Sweet and Sour Soup

The mung bean sprouts incorporated in this soup are popular in Asian cooking. They are larger than soybean sprouts and have a deeper color, nuttier taste and crunchier texture. The mung bean is considered a "cooling" food in the Asian culture and is known to be good for the liver. With the variety of sprouts and veggies in this soup, the entire spectrum of daily vitamin and mineral requirements will be met with taste and satisfaction.

1 cup (250 ml) **Brussels sprouts, quartered**

2 tbsp sesame seed oil

2 cloves garlic, minced

1 cup (250 ml) **onion, diced**

1 cup (250 ml) **shiitake mushroom, sliced**

1 cup (250 ml) **carrot, diced**

1 cup (250 ml) **baby corn, cut ½"** (1 cm)

1 cup (250 ml) **yellow bell pepper, sliced**

1 cup (250 ml) **sweet potato, diced**

2 cups (500 ml) **vegetable stock**

2 tbsp apple cider

1 tbsp honey

1 tbsp tamari

1 tsp miso

1 cup (250 ml) **soybean sprouts**

1 cup (250 ml) **mung bean sprouts**

¼ cup (60 ml) **green onion**

Watercress, for garnish

In a large pot of boiling salted water, blanch the Brussels sprouts for 3 minutes. Drain and immediately rinse in cold water.

Heat oil over medium heat and sauté garlic, onion, mushrooms, carrots, corn, pepper and sweet potato until soft. Add vegetable stock, apple cider, honey and tamari; cook for 10 minutes. Stir in Brussels sprouts, miso, sprouts and green onion, then garnish with watercress and serve immediately.

Serves 2

Brussels Sprouts
This odd looking vegetable apparently originated in Brussels, hence the name Brussels sprout. However, I like the German's interpretation of Rosenkohl, which when translated means "rose cabbage." No matter what you call them, this vegetable is an excellent winter food, and perfect for a tasty soup. They are an excellent source of vitamins C and A, phosphorus and calcium.

Essene Bread

This is an adaptation of the original Essene bread, which was baked on stones in the desert. Baking at a low temperature preserves most of the nutritional value of the sprouts. Naturally sweet, this is the answer to avoiding sugary foods and snacks.

1 ½ cups (375 ml) **wheat berries**

Soak wheat berries for 12 hours and sprout them according to the "Basic Sprouting Method" (page 23). As soon as the basic sprout has formed and is about ¼" (5 mm) long, remove them to make the bread.

Let the sprouts dry a little. Grind the sprouts in a blender, food processor or grain mill until they become a lumpy mush. Turn sprouts out onto a clean surface and knead the mush for about 10 minutes. Form into a round, flat loaf 6" to 8" (15 to 20 cm) across and 2" to 3" (5 to 8 cm) high.

Use a metal pie pan with holes in the bottom for ventilation.

Place loaf in the pan and bake on low in a slow cooker for 8 to 10 hours. I put an upside down bowl in the bottom of the cooker so that the bread is in the middle of the pot and the heat gets evenly distributed. Do not cover it as this will prevent excess moisture from escaping and make the bread too wet. Use a damp knife to cut the bread.

Variation 1: after kneading the grain mush, add ½ cup (125 ml) currants, small raisins or other organic dried fruit and form into the loaf.

Variation 2: use rye, oat, barley or a combination of these sprouts instead of the wheat berries. Only wheat needs to be kneaded, but it doesn't hurt to knead the others a little to mix the sprouts together.

Variation 3: add ¼ cup (60 ml) each of chopped sunflower seeds or almond sprouts and organic dried fruit.

Makes 1 loaf

Pan Tip
If you don't have a pie pan with holes in the bottom (found in kitchenware stores) make your own from an aluminum pie pan. Poke the holes from the inside of the pan so that any rough edges will be on the outside.

Essene Bread Pie Crust
Use this no-fat, no-sugar pie crust for no-bake pies.

Thinly slice the Essene bread using a wet knife. Put slices in a pie pan and press the edges together with wet fingers to make a uniform crust. Bake in the oven at 325°F (160°C) for 10 to 20 minutes or until firm, depending on the moisture content of the bread.

Walnut-Sprout Bread

This wonderful recipe makes a one-pound (500 g) loaf. Consult your bread machine recipe book for directions if you have a larger machine. You can find coconut milk powder in Asian or health food stores. The incredible combination of walnuts and sprouts will make this bread a favorite.

½ **cup walnuts, crumbled**

1 ¼ **tsp dry yeast**

1 **tbsp coconut milk powder**

2 ¼ **cups** (560 ml) **organic whole wheat bread flour** (for bread machines)

3 **tbsp natural sugar**

1 **tsp sea salt**

1 **tbsp extra-virgin olive oil**

1 **cup** (250 ml) **lukewarm water** (80°F or 27°C)

⅔ **cup** (165 ml) **chopped sunflower, mung bean or sesame seed sprouts**

Place all ingredients, except for sprouts, in the bread machine in the above order. Set machine for whole wheat or light cycle. When signal sounds for adding nuts and fruit, add the sprouts. When done, immediately remove from pan and cool on a rack.

Makes 1 loaf

For more tasty and nutritious bread recipes read *Healthy Breads for the Breadmaker* by Silke Alles and Sieglinde Janzen (*alive* Natural Health Guide #13, 2000)

48

mung bean

Ruben Sprout Sandwich

Filled with the lively taste of raw sprouts and rich flavor of mushrooms, these sprout buns make an unforgettable Ruben sandwich.

Sprout Buns:

1 cup (250 ml) **unbleached flour** (or bread flour)

⅓ cup (80 ml) **whole wheat flour**

1 tbsp baking powder

1 tbsp natural sugar or honey

2 tbsp + 1 tsp rolled oats

¼ cup (60 ml) **roasted water chestnuts or other nut, freshly ground**

1 ½ cups (375 ml) **Gruyère or Provolone cheese, grated**

⅔ cups (165 ml) **mung bean sprouts, chopped**

2 egg whites

2 tbsp extra-virgin olive oil

¾ cup (185 ml) **whole milk**

1 tbsp butter, to grease muffin cups

Filling:

2 cups (500 ml) **shiitake, Portobello or white mushrooms, sliced**

2 tbsp extra-virgin olive oil

1 tsp tomato paste

1 tsp honey

1 tsp paprika

1 tbsp mayonnaise

2 slices Swiss cheese

1 ripe Beefsteak tomato, sliced

2 cups (500 ml) **alfalfa sprouts**

Vegetable salt or Herbamare, to taste

Preheat oven to 375°F (190°C). Grease 6 large muffin cups with butter.

Buns: Combine flours, baking powder, sugar, 2 tablespoons of rolled oats and ground nuts. Stir in cheese and mung beans. In a small bowl, combine egg white, oil and milk. Add liquid mixture to dry ingredients, stirring until just moistened. Fill greased muffin cups three-quarters full then sprinkle with remaining rolled oats. Bake for 30 minutes. Remove from oven and cool on a rack.

Sandwich: Sauté mushrooms in oil over medium heat for 5 minutes or until golden brown.

Combine tomato paste, honey, paprika and mayonnaise; spread onto the cut buns. Layer with mushrooms, cheese, tomato and sprouts.

Serves 2

Alfalfa-Bocconcini Croutons

This variation of an old favorite will be a hit with guests and the whole family. In addition to ample vitamins, minerals and enzymes, alfalfa sprouts contain sterols that lower cholesterol and strengthen the immune system, and chlorophyll that controls hot flashes and supports hormonal functions.

4 slices walnut-sprout bread (page 48) **or whole grain bread**

1 large avocado, diced

1 tsp fresh lemon juice

¼ cup (60 ml) **green onion, diced**

1 clove garlic, minced

2 cups (500 ml) **alfalfa sprouts, divided**

2 pieces bocconcini, cut in half

1 large ripe tomato, sliced

1 cup (250 ml) **radish, julienned**

Place bread in a baking dish and toast on each side under the broiler.

Meanwhile, combine avocado, lemon juice, green onion and garlic in a bowl. Remove bread from oven and spread avocado mixture on each slice of bread. Cover with sprouts and top with cheese. Place the baking dish 6" (15 cm) below broiler until the cheese melts.

Arrange tomato, radish and alfalfa onto plates and place croutons around.

Serves 2

red radish

green onion

Alfalfa Sprouts
The always-popular alfalfa sprout is popular for good reason. This live, fresh food is high in minerals, protein, and vitamins A, B complex, C, D, E and K.

Antipasto with Mixed Sprouts

"Anti" means "before" in Italian and hence antipasto is usually an appetizer served before pasta, the main course. This particular antipasto is wonderful with any kind of rye or whole grain bread. The delicious taste of eggplant in this recipe adds the perfect substance to an already nutritious, unique experience.

1 large white onion

4 slices eggplant

2 tbsp + 2 tbsp extra-virgin olive oil

2 tbsp balsamic vinegar

1 large tomato, sliced

2 cups (500 ml) **mixed alfalfa, sunflower or sprouts of your choice**

½ cup (125 ml) **black olives**

½ cup (125 ml) **feta cheese, crumbled**

Herbamare, to taste

Peel the onion and trim the long strands of roots, leaving the root stem intact. Quarter the onion. Heat 1 tablespoon of oil in a pan over medium heat and panfry the onion until golden brown. Panfry the eggplant separately in 1 tablespoon of oil until both sides are golden brown.

In a small bowl, whisk together oil and vinegar. Place sprouts onto plates, arrange eggplant on top, tomatoes on the side, sprinkle with cheese and olives and drizzle with the oil and vinegar.

Serves 2

white onion

Elegant Eggplant
The lovely eggplant is a favorite ingredient in vegetarian dishes. Their fleshy texture make them a versatile ingredient and their nutritional value a good choice as well. This low-calorie food (technically a berry, not a vegetable) is an excellent source of folic acid and is available year round in grocery stores.

Fettuccine
with Sprouts and Grape Tomatoes

This perfectly delicious and healthy pasta dish is guaranteed to lift your spirits and your energy with its combination of complex carbohydrates, complete proteins, vitamins, minerals and enzymes. Designed for health and taste, this dish also serves as a gourmet meal, if you wish to share it.

7 oz (200 g) **whole grain fettuccine**

¼ cup (60 ml) **onion, chopped**

2 cloves garlic, minced

¼ cup (60 ml) **extra-virgin olive oil**

1 ½ cups (375 ml) **mixed lentil, chick pea, bean or alfalfa sprouts**

¼ cup (60 ml) **black olives**

¼ cup (60 ml) **grape tomatoes**

½ cup (250 ml) **Brussels sprouts, quartered**

Sea salt and fresh ground pepper, to taste

2 tsp fresh dill, chopped

Fresh Parmesan cheese, shaved

Cook pasta in a large pot of boiling salted water; drain and set aside. Blanch Brussels sprouts in a pot of boiling salted water for 3 minutes. Drain and immediately rinse in cold water; set aside.

In a large pan, sauté onion and garlic in oil over medium heat until soft then mix in Brussels sprouts, tomatoes, olives. Add pasta, dill, sprouts, salt and pepper; toss well. Place onto plates, sprinkle with Parmesan and serve.

Serves 2

Brussels sprout

Why Settle for Less?
Why buy the regular white pasta everyone else does? It's processed to the point of having no nutritional value. If fact, it's empty calories! Choose whole wheat pasta, which is now available in most large chain grocery stores; or treat yourself to another type of whole grain pasta from your health food store or specialty shop.

Stirfried Vegetable
Sprout Cabbage Wrap

The secret to a successful stir fry is to cut vegetables into just the right sizes and add them in proper order so they are all done at the same time. The cabbage and soybean sprouts can go in at the same time, just before removing from heat. They should be slightly wilted yet crisp when served.

1 medium sweet onion, sliced

6 mushrooms, sliced

1 cup (250 ml) **carrots, julienned**

1 cup (250 ml) **zucchini, julienned**

1 cup (250 ml) **green cabbage, julienned**

2 cups (500 ml) **soybean sprouts**

2 tbsp organic coconut oil

2 tbsp corn or arrowroot starch

2 tbsp + ½ cup (125 ml) **cold water**

2 tbsp tamari

2 cloves garlic, minced

2" (5 cm) **piece fresh ginger, grated**

½–1 cup (125–250 ml) **water, or more as needed**

2 large leaves green cabbage

In a large fry pan or wok, heat oil over medium heat then stir fry the vegetables in the following order one at a time: onion, mushrooms, carrot, zucchini, cabbage and soybean sprouts. Wait for each ingredient to change color before adding the next one.

In a bowl, combine starch and 2 tablespoons of cold water to make a smooth paste then stir in tamari, ½ cup (125 ml) of cold water, garlic and ginger. Push the vegetables to the edge and up the sides of the wok or pan leaving a clear spot in the middle of the pan. Pour in the sauce and let it cook until it begins to thicken and become clear. Immediately stir in more water, then mix the vegetables into the sauce. Stir until thick and sauce is clear, not cloudy. Remove from heat and let cool.

To assemble the wrap, place cabbage leaves on a clean, flat surface. Fill with vegetables and roll, tucking in the bottom edge.

Serves 2

zucchini

Four-Sprout Tacos
with Green Tomato Salsa

It's important to eat raw food each day to replenish your supply of enzymes, which are especially abundant in sprouts. Give the tacos an extra kick and at the same time detoxify by using spicy sprouts like radish, daikon or coriander.

Tacos:

4 taco shells

1 cup (250 ml) **cherry tomatoes, cut in half**

1 cup (250 ml) **yellow bell pepper, julienned**

2 cups (500 ml) **mixed soybean, sunflower, pumpkin and alfalfa sprouts**

Salsa:

1 cup (250 ml) **green tomatoes, finely diced**

¼ cup (60 ml) **red or yellow bell pepper, finely diced**

¼ cup (60 ml) **cilantro, chopped**

¼ cup (60 ml) **onion, finely diced**

2 cloves garlic, minced

3 tbsp extra-virgin olive oil

2 tbsp fresh lemon juice

To make the salsa, thoroughly combine the ingredients in a bowl and refrigerate for 1 to 2 hours before serving, in order for the flavors to incorporate.

To assemble the tacos, fill the shells with tomato, pepper and sprouts. Serve with the salsa and a dollop of kefir or sour cream.

Serves 2

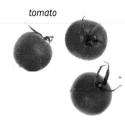

tomato

red bell pepper

American Journal of Clinical Nutrition, June 1999

Balch, James F. and Phyllis Balch. *Prescription for Nutritional Healing.* Garden City Park, NY: Avery Publishing Group, 1997.

Baldinger, Kathleen. *The World's Oldest Health Plan.* Lancaster, PA: Starburst Publishers, 1994.

Cichoke, Anthony J. *The Complete Book of Enzyme Therapy.* Garden City Park, NY: Avery Publishing Group, 1999.

Johns Hopkins University School of Medicine. *Proceedings of the National Academy of Sciences,* September 1998

Journal of Biological Chemistry, February 1999

Journal of the American Medical Association, volume 282, 1999

sources

for seeds:

Richters
Goodwood, ON
L0C 1A0 Canada
www.richters.com
Richters sells only organically
grown seeds and herbs.

Sproutamo
P.O. Box 17
Lake Mills, WI 53551
Tel: (920) 648-3853
Fax: (920) 648-2115
Email:
ezsprout@gdinet.com

for sprouters:

**Back To Basics
Products, Inc.**
11660 South State Street
Draper, UT 84020-9455
Tel: (801) 571-7349
This brand is sold in most
health food stores.

for organic seeds and sprouters:

New Natives
P.O. Box 1413
Freedom, CA 95019
(831) 728-4136
www.newnatives.com

Harvest Basket Seeds
907 Columbia Road
Fort Collins, CO 80525
www.harvestbasket.com

The Sprout House
17267 Sundance Drive
Ramona, CA 92065
Tel: (760) 788-4800
Fax: (760) 788-7979
Email:
info@SproutHouse.com

Sproutman
P.O.Box 1100
Great Barrington, MA
01230
Tel: (413) 528-5200
Fax: (413) 528-5201
Email:
Sproutman@Sproutman.com

Teldon of Canada Ltd.
7434 Fraser Park Drive
Burnaby, BC V5J 5B9
Phone: (604) 436-0545
Orders: 1-800-663-2212
Fax: (604) 435-4862
E-mail: teldon@ultranet.ca
www.teldon.ca

Miracles Exclusive
64 Seaview Blvd.
Port Washington, NY
11050 USA
Tel: (516) 621-3333
1-800-645-6360
Fax: (516) 621-1997
Email:
miracle-exc@juno.com

Remedies and supplements mentioned in this book are
available at quality health food stores and nutrition centers.

First published in 2000 by
alive **books**
7436 Fraser Park Drive
Burnaby BC V5J 5B9
(604) 435–1919
1-800–661–0303

© 2000 by *alive* books

Book Design:
    Liza Novecoski
Artwork:
    Terence Yeung
    Raymond Cheung
Food Styling/Recipe Development:
    Fred Edrissi
Photography:
    Edmond Fong
    (except when credited otherwise)
Photo Editing:
    Sabine Edrissi-Bredenbrock
Editing:
    Sandra Tonn
    Julie Cheng

Canadian Cataloguing in
Publication Data

Kathleen O'Bannon CNC
    Sprouts

(*alive* Natural Health Guides, 30
ISSN 1490-6503)
ISBN 1-55312-026-4

Printed in Canada